Views of the cathedral over the walls of the Jardín Arqueológico.

The Roman regions suffered various Barbarian invasions over the course of the 3rd century. In those times of pillaging and looting, the story of two now sanctified heroes, Feliu and Narcís, forms a summary of the chronicles of a time and a religion, the Christian faith, which soon made its triumphant entry into Roman *Gerunda.* In the 8th century, the troops of Ludovic Pious entered Girona, subjecting the township to the laws of "committees" which decided to convert it into city-earldom, along with other northern enclaves, forming the Marca Hispánica which defended the possessions of Char-

lemagne. Then followed the strife between Christians and Saracens, though Girona suffered its effects but little, as most of the fighting took place further south. Fruit of the city's privileged geographic location was notable expansion, with the creation of *barrios,* quarters, clustering around, and soon surpassing, the city walls. This relative tranquillity also favoured the flourishing of a notable community of Jewish traders, thanks to whom the Cabalistic school of the philosopher Bonastruc Ça Porta was set up. The next period of conflict to affect Girona was during the war between France and the

Aragonese armies of Peter the Great. And, though the city put up a stoic resistance, and the destruction of its walls and the decimation of its soldiers, this must have been an enclave of great repute, for Queen Joan, mother of the future Catholic King, Ferdinand, took refuge within its walls when, in the 14th century, and with John II on the throne, the cruel Wars of Aragon took their bloody place in history.

After the discovery of America in 1492, Mediterranean interests gave way to those of the Atlantic, whilst Barcelona began to centralise power in the region, relegating Girona once more to a secondary role. Conflict with the French broke out again in 1675, now with the troops of Louis XIV, the Sun King, who twice laid siege to the city, and once more in Napoleonic times during the War of Spanish Succession. Its heroic resistance to the French armies won Girona the title of "Three Times Immortal City". These warlike confrontations continued until the struggle against the government of Espartero, when the Catalan General Prim surrounded the city in a battle involving a third enemy this time, a natural one, as a great storm made the River Ter burst its banks, causing enormous loss of life and property.

Cloister of the Benedictine Monastery of Sant Pere de Galligants.

Fragment of "The Flood and Noah's Arc" on one of the capitals in the cathedral.

However, conflict and battle gradually gave way to peaceful development until in the middle of the last century, thanks to industrialisation, Girona once more began to enjoy expansion. The city grew beyond its medieval walls, communications were improved by the railway links established, firstly with Barcelona and, later, with France. All this led to the flourishing of the textile industry in Girona itself and in the entire region. Economic expansion, in turn, favoured a period of rebirth of Catalan culture, of which Girona, along with Figueres, were important centres.

Figueres, capital of the Alt Empordà *comarca,* was the last seat of the Parliament during the Republic). Nowadays, Girona, though still breathing that air of a peaceful city, boasts one of the best-conserved historic centres in Catalonia, containing traces of Moorish, medieval, Jewish, Romanesque, Gothic and Modernist elements. Not only is this a rich area of architectural heritage, however, it is also the scene of many of the daily activities of the city.
A city situated between the Guilleríes and Gavarras mountains, capital of the Gironès comarca of Catalonia,

Girona is a place of transit between the peaks and valleys of the Pyrenees and the Mediterranean sea where, thanks to the beautiful beaches of the Costa Brava, tourism has become one of the main motors of the local economy. A relaxed stroll through time which, accompanied by this guide, gives us the chance to make a thorough visit to the still-beating heart of what was originally Roman *Gerunda*.

A view of the city of Girona, crossed by the River Onyar.

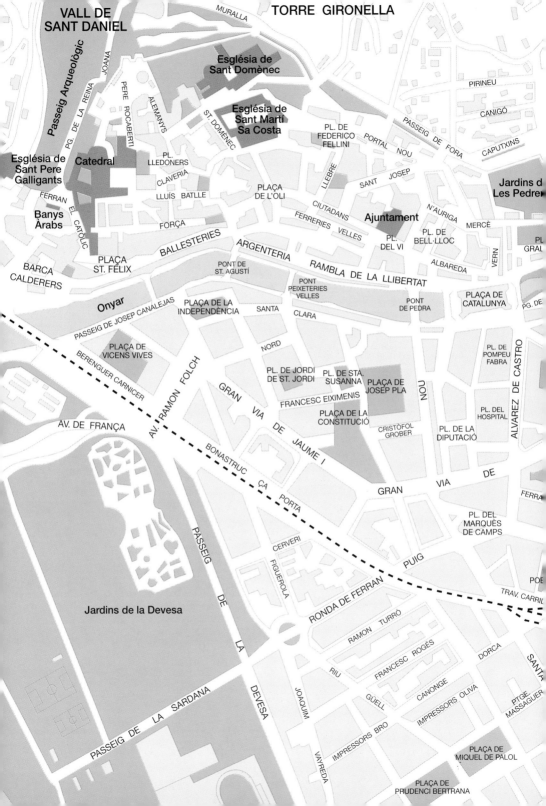

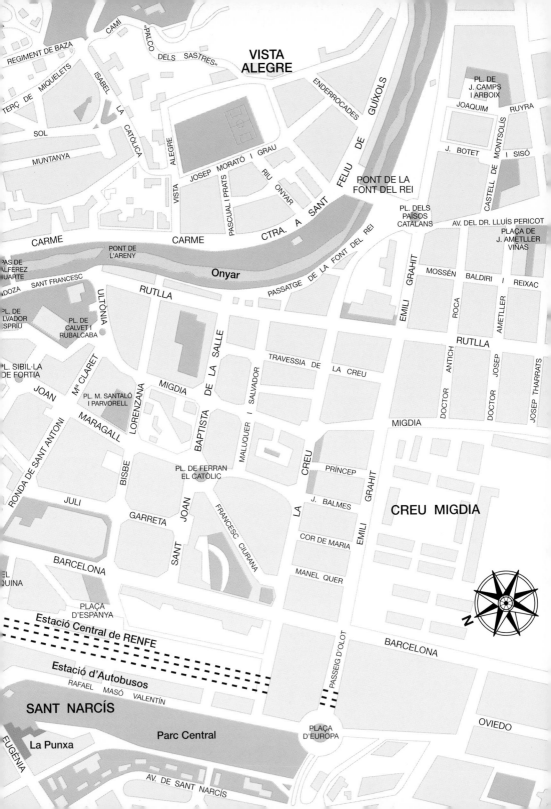

Girona Cathedral, presiding over the city.

The cathedral square with the steps leading into the building.

THE VISIT TO GIRONA

1.- The Cathedral of Santa María

Two prominent towers form Girona's best-known silhouette. One of these is the neoclassical belltower of **Girona Cathedral,** which rises above the rest of the city, firstly due to its position on the top of the gentle hill on which the city stands, but also due to the pilaster on which the cathedral rests, making it rise practically at the same height as the surrounding rooftops. Girona cathedral was built over the remains of an earlier Visigoth cathedral and was consecrated in 1038. The building is

a compendium of riches conferred on it by the successive architectural styles which have contributed to its present appearance.

We begin our visit from the broad open space formed by **Plaça de la Catedral,** which square is flanked on all sides by an interesting series of constructions and styles. The cathedral front, designed as an altarpiece in stone, presides over the scene, whilst on the other side is the **Gothic Palace of the Pia Almoina and l'Ardiaca.** Opposite is one of the finest noble palaces in the entire city, which now houses the justice administration. Before the cathedral is

a wide 18th-century stairway completed the Baroque site. This is one of the broadest main cathedral entrances in Europe, its 90 steps elevating the building so that it looks down on all the other palaces in the square. The history of Girona Cathedral is full of ups and downs. Whilst it took just 16 years to complete the first construction under the patronage of Count Ramón III, who intended to grant all privileges, work was interrupted for a lengthy period

The stone altarpiece which adorns the main front of the cathedral.

Detail of the main doorway, decorated with wrought iron forms.

four centuries later due to the failure of the architects concerned to reach agreement: some argued that the cathedral should have the traditional nave and two aisles, whilst others supported the innovative concept of forming a single inner space. The final solution resulted in the construction of what was, with its 50 metre length and its width of 23 metres, "the widest nave in European Gothic architecture and the second-widest in any style, after the Basilica of Saint Peter in Rome". The façade of Girona Cathedral, which was completed in the 17th century, was extended in the 18th with the installa-

tion of various decorative elements and again in the 20th century with that of the Biblical statutes which preside it. These represent such personages as the Virgin and the Apostles, forming a magnificent, unusual stone mural on the cathedral front, one of the finest works of Catalan Baroque art. This entire frontal is crowned by an octagonal belltower in neoclassical style, which can be seen from all points of the city. At one side is the **Door of the Apostles,** thus known as it featured terra cotta figures of the Apostles, lost during the Spanish Civil War (1936-39). Climbing up the three flights of 30

Altarpiece of the High Altar, in silver plate and decorated with enamels.

The huge inner space of the cathedral. ▷

steps, admiring close-up the above-described cathedral front, we pass through the main doorway, adorned with polychromes and floral orna-mentation, into the vast, silent nave. On entering, the visitor cannot fail to be impressed by the wide space which opens up before him or her, and which seems to be supported as if by magic. No column impedes the view, nor pillars sustaining huge blocks of stone. The solution take the form of flying buttresses and ribs which spring from fine columns in the walls, supporting the majestic vault which distributes its huge weight

over this spider's web so that its immensity rests on the side walls of the building. There is but little day-light in the cathedral, just that which filters through the **stained-glass windows** (14th-16th centuries), the most interesting of which are those over the **High Altar.** These rose win-dows are the oldest preserved in the Catalan medieval style. The altar-piece presiding over the High Altar, protected by a canopy, is a Gothic work measuring 2.20 metres wide by 1.80 metres high. It is made from silver plate and enamel bas-reliefs depicting images of various saints,

Roman altar.

Chapel of the Cuatro Mártires, in one of the sides of the cathedral.

scenes from the life of Christ and of Mary, who is surrounded by Narcís and Feliu, Girona's saints. Behind the High Altar is the **Throne of Charlemagne,** an 11th-century Bishop's Throne carved from a block of white marble and decorated with floral motifs worthy of that great emperor, though it was never occupied by him. A series of chapels line the cathedral sides and the rear of the High Altar, forming an ambulatory. These contain an enormous wealth of holy treasures, as well as numerous works of great artistic interest. The most outstanding of these are the **Chapels of Sant Pere, Sant Pau, Los Cuatro Mártires de Girona** and that of **l'Assumpció de la Verge.** Another interesting element in the cathedral are the **tombs** found along its walls. The most beautifully-carved of these are those of bishops **Berenguer d'Anglasola** (14th-15th centuries) and **Bernat de Pau.** On the left as we enter the cathedral is a door leading into the **cloisters** and the dependencies containing the cathedral treasure, described below. Passing through this door, the visitor will

The cathedral cloister, surrounded by 56 pairs of columns.

Biblical scenes depicted in the cloister capitals. ▷

delight in the freshness and peace of the 12th-century cloisters, which are made up of 56 pairs of columns resting on a wall scarcely 50 centimetres high. Enjoying a relaxing walk along the passageway, we can also learn a great deal, and the decoration here has allowed historians to ascertain many things, for the capitals in the cloister depict scenes from the Old and New Testaments, but also from everyday life, portraying the trades, buildings, arts and costumes of the periods of their creation. Accompanying this artwork are the tombs of illustrious personages in their last resting-places of richly-adorned sarcophagi installed in the walls over lintels and under stone slabs in the floor. From the centre of the patio, where there is an old well at the meeting-point of four short paths, is where we can command the finest view of the tower known as the **Torre de Carlomagno,** built in the 12th century. This was formerly the belltower of the old Romanesque cathedral, but is now in disuse. It is, nevertheless, one of the few elements which remain from that original building, serving now as a flying buttress for the walls.

Tapestry of the Creation, the most valuable work in the Cathedral Museum.

The cathedral treasure

Five Chapterhouses line the cathedral cloister, three of them housing the **cathedral treasure,** a collection of pieces of incalculable value which take us back over a period of more than ten centuries, from the 10th to the 20th centuries. Of all the fine works here, the most precious, one which, for many, "justifies the visit to Girona", is that known as the Tapestry of the Creation. This, dating to the 11th and 12th centuries, is a magnificent work which was first lost for many years amongst hundreds of other religious artworks and then misused, some of its pieces used as cloths for dusting, by people unaware of its real value and importance. The tapestry, measuring a total of 12 square metres, is made from wool dyed using ochres and living colours. Full of symbolism, the centre is occupied by an image of Christ, with a very young face, just as he was represented during the first few hundred years of the history of Christianity. Around him are portrayed the Seven Days of the Creation, with allusions to Adam and Eve and Paradise. All these images are, in turn, bordered by images of archangels playing trumpets in praise of God.

Details of the drawings in the Tapestry of the Creation.

Besides these religious allegories, the tapestry also contains others alluding to the months and seasons of the year and to the most important trades, tasks and activities of the time. According to the experts, the subject-matter of the tapestry "contains clear philosophical references to Plato and his conception of the world as part of a whole, and to Aristotle's theory that the world is governed by concentric spheres".

Another of the treasures in the cathedral museum is a series of original illuminated manuscripts. All finely-made, they feature particularly the 10th-century Mozarab **Códice del**

Pages in the Codex of the Beato de Girona, on display in the Cathedral Museum.

Beato, a work transcribed by Senior, with miniatures by Emeteri and Eude and Moorish elements which remind us that, in the Middle Ages, the influence of Córdova was far-reaching, embracing the entire Peninsula. This codex alludes to the "Commentaries on the Apocalypse" made by the Beato de Liébana. This work, featuring magnificent chromatic resolution, nevertheless also reveals deficiencies in its figurative portrayal. Another fine work reminds us once more of the Moorish influence which was so strong in those times: this is the **Arc of Hixem II,** Caliph of Córdova, made from rich, finely-wrought embossed silver (10th century).

The treasure also contains silver-covered bibles (14th century), other tapestries such as that of the Adoration, the "Bible" of Charles V of Valois (15th century), gold and enamelled crucifixes, silver and inlaid crosiers, jewels, the **Monstrance of El Corpus** (20th century), reliquaries, censers, images such as that of the **Virgen de la Seo,** a 12th-century Romanesque carving, such statues as the alabaster figure of **Saint Carlemany** (14th century), venerated for centuries and in reality an image of King Peter the Ceremonious, and altarpieces and paintings from different periods. Before concluding this visit to the cathedral museum, we should pause at the Chapel de l'Esperança, which forms a dividing partition between the chapterhouses and the cloister. The **Gate of Sant Miquel,** as well as providing access to the dependencies containing the cathedral museum, also leads into this charming little church, which contains two more outstanding ornamental elements. The first of these is the sculpture of the **Dormition of Mary,** an 18th-century work which is popularly known as "the Virgin's bed", the second another tomb like those found in the cathedral proper. This is the burial-place of **Bishop Guillem de Boill,** a 16th-century sepulchre featuring a beautiful, highly natural recumbent figure.

A page from the Bible of Carlos V.

Cathedral monstrance. ▷

A cross decorated with enamels

Silver papal crosier.

Chapel of L'Esperança, in one of the cathedral annexes.

Image of Charlemagne, in the cathedral treasure.

One of the Virgins in the cathedral treasure.

Tomb of Guillen de Boill.

Detail from the Tapestry of the Annunciation.

ECCE BOILLIERPETRVS NOBILI Q GVILELMVS
AMELIA PATRIA VAELLICAE REGENT
HIC PASTOR VIXIT TOT DISCRIMINE RERVM
VT REQVIESCAM BONE VIATOR ORA
M D XXXII

The Lioness of Girona, traditional starting-point for the tour of the old city.

3.- The Old City

To get off to the best possible start to our walking tour of the city, beginning in the streets around the cathedral, we should obey popular tradition and kiss the haunches of the **Lleona** (lioness) of Girona, an act reputed to bring good luck. This "Lioness" is none other than the one sculpted from a block of stone, copy of a Romanesque work, representing the animal perched atop a column opposite what is the second most important church in the city, the **Church of Sant Feliu,** whose towers (one unfinished and the other damaged by lightning) combine with the two towers of the cathedral to form an unmistakable part of the physiognomy of Girona. This Gothic church was built on the site of a Roman necropolis, and it conserves various extraordinary tombs from Roman times (2nd-4th centuries) in the chancel, embedded in the walls. These include one tomb whose decoration depicts the Rape of Proserpine. It was in this cemetery that Girona's best-loved saints, Feliu and Narcís (patron saint of the city, were buried and over which the old chapels were

Views from the cathedral of the Church of San Feliu.

built which finally gave way to the construction of the collegiate church we now see. Inside, behind the High Altar, is the alabaster sarcophagus dedicated to Saint Narcís and a Gothic recumbent Christ, carved with enormous anatomical naturalism. Nevertheless, the saint has his own chapel with an arched entrance on the left-hand side of the church, and it is there where his relics rest, in a silver sarcophagus. We can com-

Interior of the Gothic Church of San Feliu.

Square in front of the Monastery of Sant Pere de Galligants.

Apse of Sant Pere de Galligants.

plete our visit to the Church of Sant Feliu by admiring the **Monument to the Heroines of Saint Barbara** and the small **Parish Museum.**

Going northwards from Plaça de Sant Feliu we come to **Plaça de Sant Pere,** beside the Galligants River. This square conserves all the charm with which it was rehabilitated in the middle of the last century, and it is here that we find one of the most outstanding works of Catalan Romanesque art: the Benedictine **Monastery of Sant Pere de Galligants,** built in the 12th century, though it contains various features from ear-

lier periods, such as the façade, which contains fine carvings and archivolts. By contemplating its octagonal belltower and the site as a whole, we can gain an idea of how prosperous Girona must have appeared during the Middle Ages. The monastery has magnificent cloister which, though small, boasts magnificent capitals carved with Biblical figures and animals, as well as a large number of Jewish tombstones, brought here from the nearby Jewish cemetery on Mount Montjuïc. The riches of Sant Pere de Galligants are completed by an **Archaeological Museum,** which

exhibits items discovered in the city ranging from the Paleolithic to the Visigoth periods. The same tiny square contains the modest but important Romanesque **Chapel of Sant Nicolau,** where early Christian elements have been discovered. Leaving the square, which lies at one end of the old city, we take one of its narrow thoroughfares, Carrer de Ferran El Católic, which leads us back to the centre and where we can visit the **Moorish Baths,** really Christian, though with Moorish elements. Such baths fulfilled an important role in protecting public health in such a period as the Middle Ages, when washing facilities did not abound. In fact these are the only Christian baths found in the entire Peninsula and are one of only three of their kind in Europe. The site consists of a hall and rooms for washing and for conversing. Refreshed after our visit to these baths, we continue to walk southwards to enter the relaxing walled enclosure surrounding the cathedral. This is the **Paseo Arqueológico de Girona,** an "Archaeological Walk" which leads us to a 14th-century defensive tower, the Torre Gironella, which offers fine

Cloister of Sant Pere de Galligants,
with finely-carved capitals.

The Romanesque Chapel of San Nicolau.

Exterior of the Moorish Baths.

views of Sant Pere de Galligants and the Sant Daniel Valley. From here we can retrace our steps, via the Portal de Sobreportes (built in the 11th century over the still-visible base of a Roman door) to Plaça de la Catedral once more before entering the Jewish Quarter. It was in the cathedral and surrounding area where the monumental area of the Vella Força once stood, the original thoroughfare which led to the creation of Roman *Gerunda*. Here we find **Plaça de los Apóstoles,** which forms part of the portal of the same name, extending from the cathedral side where the

cemetery formerly lay. This esplanade, containing the fountain known as the **Fuente de la Pera,** is flanked by, on the one side, the walls of the **Casa de l'Ardiaca** and, opposite and on a higher level, the **Museu d'Art de Girona.** This City Art Museum is housed in the former bishop's palace, and contains works from all over Girona province which complement the collection we have already seen in the cathedral museum, featuring such outstanding pieces as the **Arc of Sant Pere de Roda,** the **Virgin of Besalú** and the **Púbol Altarpieces.** The south side of the

The well in the Moorish Baths. ▷

Gardens in Girona's Paseo Arqueológico.

Sant Pere de Galligants. ▷

square is presided over by the **Pia Almoina,** a Gothic construction combining noble and defensive elements originally built to provide shelter to the needy. To its left is the **Casa Pastors,** a noble old house now used as the Palace of Justice. This is a building featuring echoes of the Renaissance style which served as the residence of Alvarez de Castro during the Napoleonic siege. From Plaça de la Catedral, we go down the Escaleras de la Pera to Calle de la Força which was for centuries a road crossing through the walled city. As reminders of its former importance as a thoroughfare, we find it lined with fine noble palaces with beautiful, fresh entrance patios where carriages would pull up. Some of these houses continue to be used as private residences, whilst others have been adapted for the use and enjoyment of the population as a whole, converted into cafés, art galleries and antique shops, keeping alive the tradition of this street as a busy place of trade and thoroughfare.

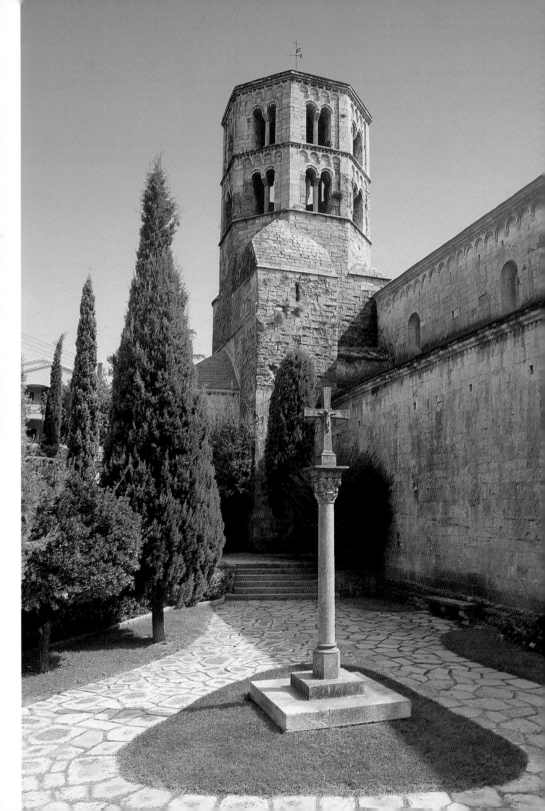

Callejón de Sant Llorenç in the Jewish Quarter.

4.- The "Call" (Jewish Quarter)

From Calle de la Força, climbing up one side of the gently sloping hill, spreads out the Jewish Quarter, known in Catalan-speaking areas as the **Call.** This is a veritable labyrinth of terraced slopes and narrow streets which, along with nearby Besalú in Girona province, formed one of the most important centres of Jewish culture during the Middle Ages. Since the confrontation between Christian and Moslem Spain was taking place further to the south, Girona's Jewish community did not only remain stable, but was even able to flourish, occupying a well laid-out quarter which has been conserved to our times. This distance from the main battlefields also meant that Girona was one of the few places which allowed its Jewish community to dwell within the city walls.

We enter the Jewish Quarter from **Callejón de Sant Llorenç,** at the start of which is a surprising modern sculpture, the work of Subirachs.

This street was where, according to popular legend, Saint Lawrence lived on his return from Rome. Here we can visit the house of **Isaac el Cec** ("the Blind"), rebuilt on the site of a synagogue, now a group of buildings standing around a restored central courtyard. The basements of some of these buildings rise straight from the rock of the hillside. A visit to the **Centre Bonastruc Ça Porta** permits us not only to admire the architecture of the time, but also to gain a vision of the heritage left by the Jewish community to this Catalan city. The community is known to have resided here from the year 890 to the expulsion of the Jews in 1492. During this time, this population of some one thousand souls earned itself a reputation thanks to its great cultural development, opening many schools where the mystical knowledge of the Cabalistic School was imparted. From the old city, there are various paths leading to the interior of the "Call", but there can be no doubt that the route which will best evoke the flavour of this quarter is the one leading to **Escalinata del Quatre Cantons,** so steep and narrow as to call to mind a time tunnel. Continuing our

Bonastruc Ça Porta Cultural Centre.

A narrow road in Girona's "Call".

The Escalinata de Sant Pere, rising up towards the cathedral.

tour of this labyrinth of these cul-de-sacs above **Calle de la Força,** we can see courtyards, large houses, their balconies adorned with wrought-iron grilles and narrow corridors, in tiny roads such as the above-mentioned **Calle de Sant Llorenç,** as well as those of **Cúndaro, Escola Pia, Clavería, Oliva I Prat, Bellmirall** or **Pujada de la Catedral.** A silent, refreshing stroll around a quarter of narrow passages and arcades which was once a bustling hive of activity, everyday life, trade and study. The **Escalinatas de la Pera** rises between

Calle de Sant Llorenç and Calle Cúndaro to **Plaça dels Apòstols,** a square adjoining the cathedral on one of the thoroughfares leading out of the quarter. These steps boast enormous architectural wealth. At their beginning is a space formerly occupied by the public baths during the time of the "Call" and converted, with the years, into cathedral administrative premises, ending in a wall where there must once have been a water cistern, crowned by a statute of the **Virgen de la Pera** (Virgin of the Pear). The quarter is even today important

City History Museum, in the former Convent of Sant Antoni.

culturally, containing, in the former **Convent of Sant Antoni,** the **City History Museum.** The museum collections include many interesting items which take us through the history of Girona, from public lighting lamps to the convent drying room where the monks' bodies were desiccated.

Virgen de la Pera, in the walls below the cathedral.

Palaces of Agullana and Caramany, in the medieval quarter of the city.

5.- Medieval quarter

As the city grew, it was obliged to expand beyond its limits, populating the area beyond the walls, creating new urban areas outside the protecting stones of the defensive system. This medieval quarter, or *Ensanche* ("expansion") is well-preserved even today, giving us a good idea of the atmosphere of the city in medieval times.

We can begin our tour of the medieval city just above the "Call", where the walls once marked the city limits and which now forms a pleasant walk along the remaining stretches of wall, commanding fine views of the old city. We shall begin our descent, then, from the very top of the walls, coming first to **Plaça de Sant Domènec,** a wide open space whose airiness contrasts with the narrow confinement of the quarter which was the subject of our previous itinerary. In this square stands the **Puerta de Rufina,** formerly one of the gates providing entrance to the walled city. The gate leads into another square, **Plaça de Lledoners,** and into such narrow streets as **Calle de Alemanys and Calle de Bell Mirall.** Now a

university zone, the square forms the campus of Girona's first university, created in 1561 and housed in the **Palace of Les Aligues.**

Passing under the Arch of **Agullana,** we go down a terraced street containing some of the most beautiful Renaissance buildings in the entire city, such as the **Palaces of Caramany and Agullana.** These steps meet another coming down from the **Church of San Martí Sa Costa,** one of the oldest in Girona, in whose central niche is an image of "when the saint offers his clothes to a beggar". Having descended these steps too, we find ourselves in the very heart of the old city, where the list of interesting streets and squares is enormous. Among the most notable of these we can mention **Plaça de l'Oli** (where the well-known musician Xavier Cugat was born), branching out from which is, amongst others, **Pujada de Sant Domènec.** This rise leads into various other interesting streets, **Calle dels Ciutadans** for example, formerly the residence of many families of high descent and which contains the **Palace of La Fontana d'Or,** unquestionably the most outstanding civil building in the

Church of Sant Martí Sa Costa, one of the oldest in the city.

Fontana d'Or, a civil building of fine architectural line.

The porches of the arcades D'En Rosés.

vicinity and which is now used for exhibitions and other cultural events, though it still preserves the remains of a mill. Also interesting here are the **Palaces of Massaguer and Los Condes de Solterra.** All around, the streets and squares bear the names of the different guilds where the activities referred to once took place. Girona's beautiful medieval quarter is, in short, a web of cobbled streets running between passages and porticoes such as the **Arcada d'En Rosés.** Our tour of the quarter takes in such interesting streets as **Mercaders, Peixeteries, Abeu-** **radors, Ferreries, Argenteria,** etc, and squares such as **Plaça de les Castanyes, Plaça dels Raïms,** the smallest in Europe, or **Plaça del Vi.** This last porticoed square contains the 19th-century **Casa Carles** (thus known as it had been the residence of monarchs since the reign of Charles IV) and **Casa Barceló,** featuring reliefs of the four martyred saints of Girona: Germán, Justo, Paulino and Scici. Other interesting buildings in this quarter include the **Casa de la Ciutat** (town hall) and the **Palace of the Generalitat** (seat of the autonomous government)

Almost by the riverside now, we can stroll around the busiest of the streets of the old city, already a market as far back as the Middle Ages: this is **Rambla de la Llibertat** de **Girona,** also arcaded and full of shops, cafés and terraces. This thoroughfare leads into **Rambla de Mossèn Jacint Verdaguer,** terminating in **Plaça de Catalunya.** We can also end our tour of medieval **Girona** in this square, built over the bed of the River Onyar.

Arch of Agullana, in Las Escaleras de Sant Domènec.

Calle Mercaders, a street in the medieval quarter.

Calle Mercaders is now lined with many art galleries.

Girona Town Hall.

Rambla de la Llibertat, Girona's busiest street.

6.- The bridges over the River Onyar

One of Girona's three rivers forms a dividing partition between the old and modern cities. The Onyar is crossed by half a dozen bridges commanding views of one of the most typical sights of Girona: the **Houses of the Onyar,** built between the 17th and 20th century on the medieval walls. Formerly grey and neglected, the buildings were rehabilitated in 1983, their fronts remodelled and painted in bright colours to produce the lovely sight which meets the eye from any of the bridges. Facing the old city, from left to right, the bridges are: **the Puente d'en Gòmez; the Puente de Sant Agustí,** which leads to the crossroads of Calle Ballesteríes and Calle Argentería (parallel to the river) and Calle de la Cort; the **Puente de les Peixeteries Velles,** a metallic construction with wooden floor, built by the firm of Eiffel (which also built the famous tower in Paris), and the **Puente de Pedra,** with arcades over the river and communicating with such important thoroughfares as **Calle Santa Clara** or **Calle Sant Francesc** with the **Rambla de la Llibertat** and **Plaça Catalunya.** Further to the right beyond the city centre, the Onyar is crossed by the **Puente de l'Areny** and the **Puente de la Font del Rei.**

Houses along the River Onyar, rehabilitated in 1983.

Tourist train crossing the Puente de Pedra.

7.- The Mercadel quarter

The area around the Onyar, which runs down the rugged hill on which the quarters of the old city stand, is formed by a gentle plain on which Girona continued its expansion. This entire zone, more modern, was also once protected by walls, which followed the course of what is now **Via de Jaume I,** but these were demolished at the turn of the present century. The same is true of the medieval traces once found here, erased from the map during the industrial period, all signs of which were also, in turn, demolished to make way for a district of houses, shops and offices.

Two squares mark the beginning and end of the area covered by the Mercadel quarter. As we finished our last itinerary at the Puente de Pedra, the nearest of these is **Plaça de la Constitució,** thus known in commemoration of the approval of the Spanish Constitution. In the square is a peaceful statue of a sitting child, marking the signing of the Constitution on 6 December 1978. The model for the statue was Mar Cabeza Catalán, born that same day, at the age of thirteen.

The district is closed by the **Plaça de Santa Susana,** a square presided over by the church of the same name, one of the few historic monuments in

El Mercadel, and whose foundations reveal traces of an early Christian building. In striking architectural contrast is a tower, now converted into a museum, which was the city's first power station, which operated thanks to the current supplied by the medieval water channels. To the right is the enclosed square completing this triangle of tiny squares, this time dedicated to the Ampurdà region's most famous writer, Josep Pla.

Leaving this eclectic combination of squares, we take winding **Calle de les Hortes,** lined by many bookshops, which leads to the busy **Calle de Santa Clara.** From here, we have two options. To the left we come to **Plaça de l'Independència** (also reached by **Gran Via de Jaume I).** This square takes the form of a large open space with porticoes, following the model of most main squares in Catalan towns and cities, and contains the tallest constructions built in Catalonia during the 19th century, one of them now housing the Post Office. In the centre of the square is the monument to the defenders of Girona and by **the Fountain of the Boy and the Tortoise.**

However, if we choose to turn to the right, we follow **Calle de Santa Clara** to **Calle Nou** or the arcaded **Calle de Sant Francesc,** then taking one of the narrow streets such as that of

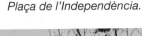

Plaça de l'Independència.

Plaça de la Diputació.

Fontanilles and **Plaça de la Diputació** to **Plaça de l'Hospital.** This square is presided over by the Baroque façades of the **Hospital de Santa Caterina,** a 17th-century building which still functions as a hospital. The building has a pleasant central courtyard with a pharmacy dating to the 17th century, displaying the typical utensils and jars. Here also is the **Hospice,** designed by the architect of the Basilica del Pilar in Saragossa, a classical building now used as the Cultural Centre and Public Library.

Façade of the Hospital of Santa Caterina.

The Farinera Teixidor and the Casa de la Punxa, two of Girona's finest Modernist buildings.

8.- Modernist and Contemporary Girona

Though they are not many in number, we should note the various Modernist buildings scattered around the city, most of them designed by the architect Rafael Masó, who made an important contribution to rehabilitating the city as a whole. The Catalan Modernist style reached its maximum splendour during the second half of the last century and the first half of the present. Near to the modern rail and bus stations in Calle Santa Eugenia is **Casa Farinera Teixidor** (1910). This has fronts finished in ceramic and glass, materials much-used by the Modernists. Almost opposite is the **Casa de la Punxa** (1918), headquarters of the local architects' association, which takes its name ("House of the Needle") from its needle-shaped tower. The **Masó House** (1911) in Calle Ballesteries has been altered, as have **Casa Batlle** (1909) in Calle Fontilles and **Casa Gispert-Sauch** (1921) in Gran Via Jaume I.

A tour of the city born in the second half of the 20th century could well begin at the **Column of the Lion,**

Plaça del Poeta Marquina.

near the city market. This monument, featuring a lion with its paw over the mouth of a cannon, was erected in homage to the heroes of the sieges of 1808 and 1809. In Calle Sant Antoni Maria Claret is the modern **Church of El Sagrada Corazon.** Another example of new urban design is the **Cruz del Término,** a monument commemorating all the old roads which have now been lost, in Plaça Maragall-Lorenzana. Plaça del Poeta Marquina features a giant-sized work in ceramic from La Bisbal, whilst Plaça del Marquès de Camps once contained one of the old city gates. In El Mercadel is the circular building housing the **Bank of Spain** (winner of the FAD architectural award in 1990).

The modern sculptures which adorn various parts of the city deserve mention appart. In El Mercadel is the work dedicated to **Josep Pla** in the square of the same name. Opposite the Hospice is one of the most famous, by Torras Monsó, made up of deformed letters placed on the ground for children to play in. In the old city, at the meeting-point of the **Escaleras de la Pera** with **Calle de la Força,** is a sculpture by Subirachs

Modern sculpture dedicated to Josep Pla.

commemorating the 600th anniversary of the polemic between the architects as to whether the cathedral should have a single nave or three. Far from the centre, in **Plaça d'Europa,** is a sculpture by Alfaro made up of a number of aluminium structures which is lit up at night to reveal its splendour. Finally, in the nearby **Par Central** is a sculpture of steel blocks.

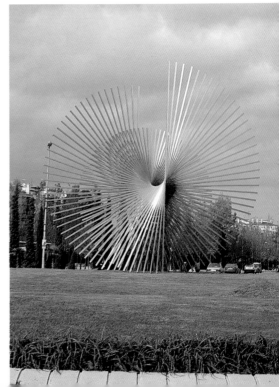

Plaça d'Europa, with a central sculpture in aluminium.

The gardens known as the Jardines de la Francesa, at the top of the city.

9.- Parks and gardens

In this chapter, we will visit some of Girona's green spaces, some larger than others, but each with its own particular importance.

Behind the cathedral, containing the Parc Arqueológic, are the **Gardens of Doctor Figueres,** whilst near the Monastery of Sant Pere de Galligants is a green area with gardens dedicated to John Lennon. In the old city are the **Gardens of La Francesa,** thus named in memory of the French lady who lived there, and, at the other end of the district, the **Gardens of the Walls,** which invite the visitor to take a gentle stroll to enjoy the fine views they command.

On the other side of the river is the most important of all, the **Parc de la Devesa,** built on the banks of the Ter by order of the occupying French during the 19th century on the site of a green space already in existence. This is the largest urban park in Catalonia, with 40 hectares containing a 19th-century garden and row upon row of plane trees, of which there are over 2,500 here.

At the confluence of the Ter and the Onyar are the **Gardens of Pedret,** which feature a sculpture representing "The birth of the life of a tree", a work considered scandalous by many. Another pleasant spot affording views over the Onyar is the promenade known as the **Paseo de Canalejas.**

Jardines de la Muralla, a promenade offering fine views over the city.

Sculpture of "The Birth of the Life of a Tree", in the Jardins de Pedret.

Jardins de la Devesa, on the banks of the River Ter.

CUSTOMS

Though it is not always easy to conserve customs, Catalonia has had the wisdom and ability to recover many of its oldest traditions, which are celebrated with great popular participation. The Sardana, the typical dance, is present at all festivities, as are the *gegants* (giants) and *cavalls* (horses), enlivening the proceedings. Fire is another element which usually plays an important role in local celebrations, either in the form of firework displays or in that of large bonfires. Catalan popular costume features a fundamental element: the barretina, a cap of Mediterranean origins. As regards architecture,

Catalonia has, fortunately, been able to recover many of its traditional farmhouses, or *masías*.

Catalan cuisine is enriched by such plates as *escudella,* pulses and vegetables stewed with meat; *empedrat,* a salad of black olives, egg and white beans: *esqueixada,* macerated cod; *mongetes amb botifarra,* white beans with the typical local sausage, and *fabes a la catalana,* kidney beans. All this accompanied by the ever-present *pa amb tomàquet* (bread spread with tomato and olive oil). Moreover, Girona boasts a variety of specialities in both sea food and mountain dishes, as well as many different types of sausage, cheese, wine, *cava* (champagne) and liqueurs.

Gegants *(giants) at the festa major in* Olot.

Fireworks in Blanes.

Simitomba, *a typical dish of the Costa Brava.*

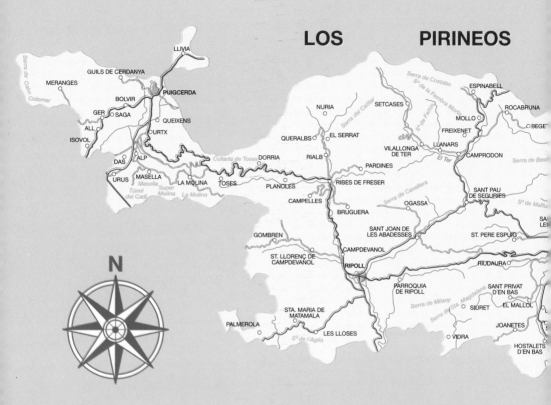

FRANC

LOS PIRINEOS

LLIVIA

GUILS DE CERDANYA
MERANGES
PUIGCERDA
BOLVIR
GER SAGA
QUEIXENS
ALL
ISOVOL
OURTX

NURIA
SETCASES
ESPINABELL
ROCABRUNA
MOLLO
BEGE
FREIXENET
QUERALBS
EL SERRAT
LLANARS
VILALLONGA
DE TER
CAMPRODON

DAS ALP
MASELLA
URUS
LA MOLINA
TOSES
Collada de Toses DORRIA
RIALB
PLANOLES
PARDINES
RIBES DE FRESER
SANT PAU
DE SEGURIES
CAMPELLES
OGASSA
BRUGUERA

GOMBREN
SANT JOAN DE
LES ABADESSES
ST. PERE ESPUIG
ST. LLORENÇ DE
CAMPDEVANOL
CAMPDEVANOL
RIPOLL
RIUDAURA

PARROQUIA
DE RIPOLL
SANT PRIVAT
D'EN BAS
EL MALLOL
SIURET

STA. MARIA DE
MATAMALA
JOANETES
PALMEROLA
LES LLOSES
VIDRA
HOSTALETS
D'EN BAS

N

PROVINCIA
DE
BARCELONA

VILADRAU

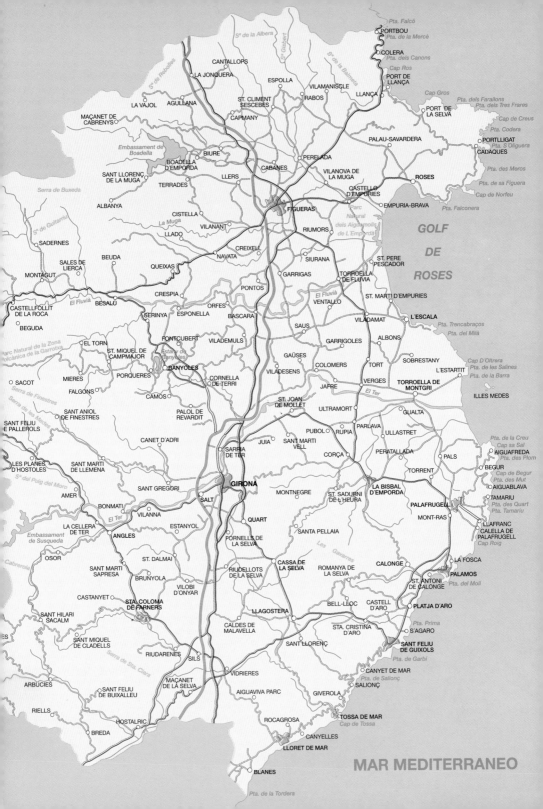

Monastery of Sant Pere de Roda, in the Alt Empordà rural district.

EXCURSIONS AROUND GIRONA

If Catalonia is one of the most beautiful regions in Spain thanks to the richness and variety of its landscapes, then Girona is, within Catalonia, a truly privileged province. Mid-way between the Pyrenean mountains and the Mediterranean coast, Girona is the ideal starting-point for a vast range of excursions, all within an hour's drive along the excellent local roads.

Towards the Pyrenees, there is a rich variety of wonderful landscapes to enjoy, as well as many artistic treasures, particularly in the form of the many Romanesque churches which populate the valleys. The proximity of the mountains mean that Girona can also boast some of the finest winter skiing resorts in the entire country, that of **La Molina** being the first to be built in Spain.

If, on the other hand, we opt to visit the Mediterranean coast, we will find few beaches in the whole world with such characteristics of those of the **Costa Brava.** From Tossa de Mar northwards, passing through the Selva, Baix Empordà and Alt Empordà rural districts, the coastline is an idyllic suc-

Costa Brava: Tossa de Mar.

Sea front along the beach at Lloret de Mar, in La Selva rural district.

cession of peaceful sandy coves, broad beaches and ragged cliffs thick with pine trees bent by the strong Tramontana winds so typical of the region.

Another option are gastronomic, ceramic or artistic routes, trying the different local specialities, admiring the fine work of the local ceramists, or visiting important places in the lives of such personalities as the writer Josep Pla or the painter Salvador Dali. There is, in fact, a fascinating Dali Route around the province, starting at the **Dali Museum** in the artist's birth-place, Figueres, as well as such other places as his home, the church where he was baptised and the place where he did his military service. The route then takes us to **Cadaqués,** where Dali had his summer residence. Along the road to this pretty seaside town of white-washed houses, we can stop at **Quermançó Castle,** which Dali painted and which fascinated him due to the many legends attached to it. Dali lived in the fishing village of **Portlligat,**

Salvador Dali Theatre-Museum in Figueres, the artist's birth-place.

The unusual façade of the Dali Theatre-Museum in Figueres.

in a house currently being converted into a museum. Already open to the public is **Púbol Castle** on the slopes of Mount Montgrí (where, at the Molí de la Torre, Dali learnt to paint). Dali acquired the mansion at Púbol, whose history is well-documented back to the 11th century, in the late-1960s as a present for his wife and muse, Gala, who lived alone there at various times. On her death (she is buried in the castle crypt), Dali moved

there himself, until a fire occurred there in 1984, after which he lived in the **Torre Galatea.** With the reorganisation complete, the **Gala-Dali Museum in Púbol** is open to the public, which can admire all the rooms and the eccentric decoration installed by this unique artist. Finally, we can complete this Dali Route by visiting the **Monastery of Els Àngels,** where the painter married Gala.

Cadaqués and Portlligat, two towns chosen by Dali as his place of residence.

A view of the Gala-Dali House-Museum, adjoining the church in Púbol.

Entrance to the residence of Dali and Gala in Púbol, now a museum.

The Shield Room contains many decorative elements installed by Dali.

CONTENTS

EDITORIAL ESCUDO DE ORO, S.A.
I.S.B.N. 84-378-1895-8
Printed by FISA - Escudo de Oro, S.A.
Dep. Legal B. 33613-2000

Romanesque cross in the cathedral walls.

Torre de Carlomagno, the now disused belltower of the old Romanesque cathedral.

GIRONA: HISTORICAL BACKGROUND

Lying amidst a splendid landscape close to the mountains of the Pre-Pyrenees on the one side and the Mediterranean coast on the other, **Girona** was born thanks to its strategic location as an enclave along the Via Augusta, built in these lands by the Romans. As an important crossroads and stopping-place, the city prospered due to the wealth brought to it as a meeting-point of peoples, trade and cultures, and suffered through the jealousy of those same peoples, who left their mark on the now hundreds of years old walls. It was the Roman conquerors who first saw the benefits of building a fortified town on the hill dominating the confluence of four rivers, the Ter, the Onyar, the Güell and the Galligants, transport and communication channels of immense importance in those times. And so, on the road linking Roman Tarraco and Barcino with what is now French Narbonne, humble *Gerunda* sprang up on the site of a tiny Iberian settlement and fortress.

W9-CTJ-070

GIRONA

Editorial Escudo de Oro, S.A.